Reading STREET

Grade **3**

Scott Foresman

Take-Home
Decodable Readers

PEARSON

Scott Foresman

Editorial Offices: Glenview, Illinois • Parsippany, New Jersey • New York, New York
Sales Offices: Boston, Massachusetts • Duluth, Georgia • Glenview, Illinois
Coppell, Texas • Sacramento, California • Mesa, Arizona

3 4 5 6 7 8 9 10 V084 14 13 12 11 10 09 08 07 06

Contents

A Winter Picnic

Written by Beth Banlin
Illustrated by Matt Sinter

Phonics Skill

Short Vowel; medial consonants in syllable pattern VCCV

dinner	suggest	picnic	basket	plastic
winter	mittens	button	traffic	napkin

Rose tells Molly, Mom, and Jane to sit by the fire. "It will make you warm."

It is time for dinner. Molly takes out plastic plates. Jane takes a napkin, cup, and fork.

"Good food and friends!" Rose smiles.

"It is not just supper," said Molly. "It is a winter picnic!"

8

Molly Wade liked Rose Hansen. Rose always waved as Molly waited for the bus.

"Jane," said Molly, "I would like to ask Rose for dinner."

"It is so cold," Jane said. "Rose will not go out on a cold winter night.

It is hard for Rose to get around when it is slick. She has to use a cane."

2

Rose Hansen smiles. "Come in! You all must be cold. Are you wet?"

Molly smiles. "We have food. Can we eat by the fire?"

7

Molly finds Mom at the stove. Corn is in a pot, and hot ham is in a pan. Mom cuts a carrot and puts it on a plate. Mom has made plum pie. Yum!

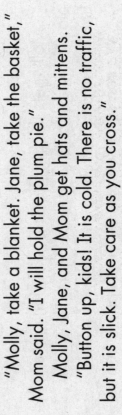

"Molly, take a blanket. Jane, take the basket," Mom said. "I will hold the plum pie."

Molly, Jane, and Mom get hats and mittens. "Button up, kids! It is cold. There is no traffic, but it is slick. Take care as you cross."

Molly raps on the door.

"Are you sad, Molly?" Mom asks.
"No, Mom, but Rose might be sad. She is alone and cannot come here for dinner."
"We can go to Rose," Mom and Jane suggest.
"We can fill a picnic basket and take it to Rose. We can eat with her. We can make a picnic happen."

Molly gets the big picnic basket. Jane puts in plastic plates, forks, and cups. Mom fills it with ham, corn, and carrots.
"We can surprise Rose. A winter picnic in a warm home will be fun."

Lunch at the State Park

Written by Sean Kenton
Illustrated by Lily Moran

Phonics Skill

Plurals -s, -es, with and without spelling change: y to i

| lunches | miles | plants | ladybugs | inches |
| babies | bunnies | flies | boxes | grapes |

Tiny fish swim in the lake. Jan and Sam wade in. Jan bends to get a fish. Oh! Oh! Jan sits in the lake. Sam and Mom get her up. Jan is wet, but the hot sun gets her dry.

Boxes and bags are in the basket. It is time to go. Mom holds the basket. Sam and Jan hold hands as they go to the car. Mom, Sam, and Jan had the best lunch ever.

16

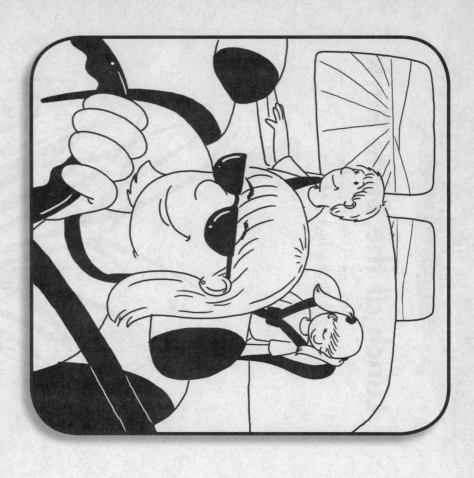

"Lunches are in the basket. The basket is in the car. Hop in! It is time to go," Mom tells Jan and Sam.

On the ride, Jan rests. Mom and Sam see things as Mom drives. Mom and Sam see farms and miles and miles of corn.

At the lake, frogs eat flies. Lines of ants take bits of food to their hills. It is time for lunch at the lake.

At the lake, Mom, Sam, and Jan sit on the blanket. Sam and Jan take the boxes and bags Mom has for them. Dishes hold grapes. Yum.

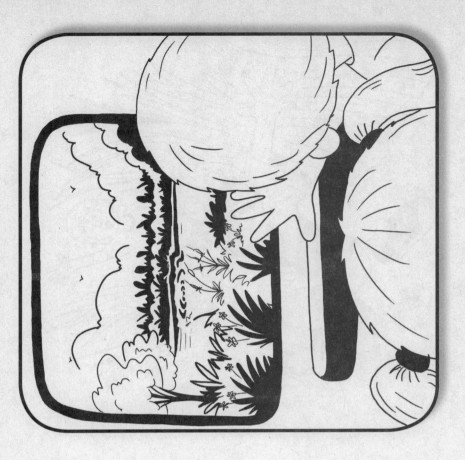

Sam asks, "Will we get there by ten?"
Mom nods yes as Jan wakes up. "Are we there
yet? Is it time for lunch?"

"Not yet," Mom tells Jan. "But you will like the
State Park. It has many plants. It has grasses and
bushes. It has lakes. Lots of animals have homes
in the park."

Rabbits hop in the grass. Jan and Sam see
babies. One, two, . . . five bunnies hop.
"Is that a dog, Mom?" asks Jan.
"No, Jan, it is a fox. Lots of foxes live here.
"Most often we do not see foxes. They nap in the
day and hunt at night."

Sam and Jan run. Mom yells, "Stop! Do not go yet. I need to get the basket. Then we will hike together."

"Will we see animals, Mom?" Jan asks.

"Yes, we will see tiny bugs and big animals too."

12

"Ladybugs! Ladybugs!" Jan holds a ladybug.

"Mom, it is red like the buds on the bushes."

Bugs jump in the grass just inches from Sam. "They sure can jump high!"

13

Teaching Bell to Behave

Written by Neil Fairbairn
Illustrated by Anna Sumptin

© Pearson Education 3

© Pearson Education 3

Phonics Skill

Base words and endings -ed, -ing, -er, est with spelling changes: double final consonant, drop final e, y to i

hopped	funniest	bigger	sitting	cried
stepped	tapped	tried	biggest	happier

It takes time for puppies to learn. But we are glad we gave Bell lessons. Bell no longer hops on laps or jumps on friends. She runs up and sits. We are happy, and Bell is happier!

24

Our puppy, Bell, hopped and jumped like a big rabbit! It was the funniest sight. But as Bell got bigger, friends did not like her jumping on them. Bell had to take lessons to behave better.

The last test was the hardest. We told Bell to sit and stay. We hid and did not let Bell see us. Bell tried to find us again and again. At last Bell just sat as she was told. She stayed. Bell got lots of bones!

We taught Bell to sit. This was not the hardest lesson for Bell. Dogs will sit if you hand them dog bones for sitting. We would hold a dog bone high up. "Sit!" Every time Bell sat, we gave our puppy a dog bone. "Good dog!" We did this lots of times. Bell was getting lots of bones.

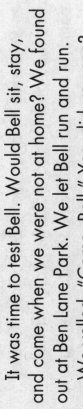

It was time to test Bell. Would Bell sit, stay, and come when we were not at home? We found out at Ben Lane Park. We let Bell run and run. We yelled, "Come, Bell." Yes, did you see? Bell came right up to us. Bell is a smart puppy!

Then we gave Bell harder lessons. Bell must stop and not go when told "Stay." We started off with sitting lessons. We made Bell sit and gave her a bone. Then we put a hand up and cried, "Stay!" We stepped away. If Bell stayed, she got dog bones. If Bell did not stay, we tapped her nose. "No, Bell, no!"

20

We were trying to make Bell come. "Come." We tried and tried to make Bell come. If Bell came, we gave her bones and made the biggest fuss. Soon Bell sat or came at our command. Bell was getting lots of bones.

21

Goat Art

Written by Angela Lowen
Illustrated by Jake Parsey

Phonics Skill

Long Vowel Digraphs ee, ea, ai, ay, oa, ow

| free | mean | train | stay | oats |
| own | feet | paint | rows | goat |

Now Mom likes Billy. "He can eat the peas, beans, and oats."
Dad likes Billy. "He is a fine goat. He pays his way."
Billy and Ann make a great pair!

32

Billy was just a kid when Ann got him. Now he is a grown goat. He is a big, bad grown goat. Billy does not mean to be bad. He just likes to get his own way. Ann tried to train Billy and keep him safe. It was a big job.

Now Ann lets Billy get in the paints. Billy paints with his feet every day. Ann sells his Goat Art. Ann takes it to art fairs. Ann sets up a display. Ann made $150 at a fair last week.

Billy did not like his pen. So Ann let him roam. Ann let him run free. Ann heard "Beep! Beep! Beep!"

"Oh, no! Billy is on the road." Ann rushed out and grabbed Billy. Ann tried to make him stay in the yard.

One day, Ann went out to paint with Billy. Ann tied him to a tree. Ann took out her paints. Billy got in them. He bit the rope and got yellow, green, and red feet. He stepped on her picture. "No, Billy, no!"

At home, a friend saw the painting. "I like it. It is different. May I take it? I will pay for it." He gave Ann $5. Yes, Billy can paint!

Billy made a meal of everything. He ate the plants in window boxes. He dug up and dined on rows of bean seeds. He feasted on grain Mom tossed to the hens. He fed on loads of hay in the barn. Mom called him "Billy the Pig."

What did Dad say about Billy? "Billy gets my goat."

"What do you mean?" Ann asked.

"I mean Billy upsets me. Billy makes me mad. Billy eats the feed. Billy gets in my way. Billy is a pain. He gets my goat!"

Ann petted Billy and patted his coat. "Billy, I am afraid that Mom and Dad will sell you. You need to be good."

Billy bleated.

Clint's Clam Chowder

Written by Chelly Bergstrom
Illustrated by Dave Lin

Phonics Skill

Vowel Diphthongs ou, ow/ou/ and oi, oy/oi/

| amounts | boiled | brown | boy | mound |
| down | Joy | choice | now | chowder |

"Wow, this is the best meal in town," Dad said when Joy gave him his big brown bowl.

"Chow down while it is hot!"

There was not a frown in the house. Mom, Dad, Joy, and Clint ate every last drop of that clam chowder. Clint was a proud boy that day!

40

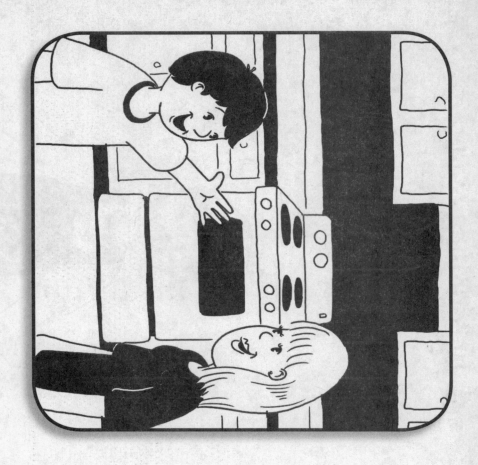

Clint had a nice plan to make supper for his mom and dad. He wanted them to be glad. Clint asked his sister Joy to help him. Joy was glad to help Clint make this fine meal for Mom and Dad.

"What is that wonderful smell?" Dad asked in a happy voice.

"Joy helped me make clam chowder!" Clint yelled, jumping up and down with glee.

"I like the sound of that," Mom added, setting down her shopping bags and hugging Clint.

"We have an hour to make supper. What will we make for Mom and Dad?" Joy asked.

"Mom likes clam chowder best," Clint said.

"That would be Dad's choice too," Joy added.

"How can we make chowder?"

"We will use our heads," Clint said.

Clint cleaned counters and scoured dishes. He set out bowls and spoons for the chowder. Then there was a loud noise outside.

"It is Mom and Dad!" Clint shouted. With a bounce in his step, Clint bounded to the front door to greet them.

Clint found the page that told them how to make the best clam chowder. Joy chopped a pound of clams. Clint added a mound of fresh things. They put in just the right amounts of cream, flour, and spices.

Joy set the big pot on the stove. When the pot of chowder boiled, the smell made Clint's mouth water.

"How long now?" Clint asked.

"We must not rush," Joy pointed out. "Good chowder takes time!"

Jason's Music

Written by Sharon Tell

Illustrated by Maura Allison

Phonics Skill

Syllable Pattern V/CV, VC/V

Jason	pupils	music	finish
rapid	focus	talent	never
even			
silent			

Loud noises from his drums filled the house day and night. But his family did not care. Mom and Dad tapped their feet. Jill hummed. Mom, Dad, and Jill were quite proud of Jason. Jason was making music again!

48

Jason had always liked music and hoped to play it well. Even as a tiny boy, Jason liked to sing and play. He pounded the keys. He even made up his own tunes. Mom and Dad asked for less noise. Jill shouted, "Stop!" But Jason did not stop. He played and played.

Ms. Bates seemed pleased. "You need to focus on drum lessons," she said. You are a good pupil. You will play drums well in no time."

Jason had lessons each week. He played rapid and slow beats on his drums. He started playing music with the class band.

Then Mom and Dad said yes. Jason could try music lessons. Jason borrowed a trumpet. Mr. Reese could give him lessons. Mr. Reese had lots of happy pupils. Jason started classes. Jason tried some notes. But horn music was not the music for him.

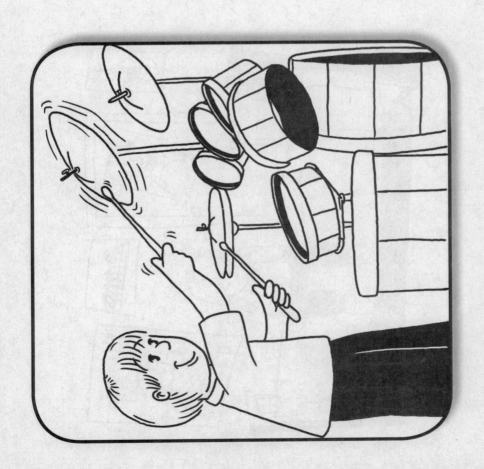
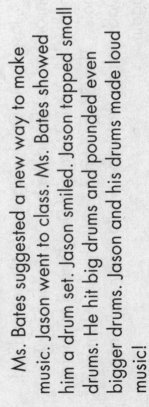

Ms. Bates suggested a new way to make music. Jason went to class. Ms. Bates showed him a drum set. Jason smiled. Jason tapped small drums. He hit big drums and pounded even bigger drums. Jason and his drums made loud music!

Jason tried to play music on a flute. His flute made odd sounds. Mrs. Lee told him, "You have so much talent. You will play well." But Jason did not finish his lessons. Flute music was not for him. He needed to play music, but not on the flute.

Jason stopped playing music. He seemed sad. Jason had not found the best music for him. The house fell silent. Mom and Dad longed for more noise. They longed for a louder house. Mom and Dad worried that Jason would never make music again.

From Farm to Table

Written by Karen Schwartz
Illustrated by Adam Corcoran

Phonics Skill
Syllable Pattern C + -le

apple	sample	table	simple	ladle
kettle	handle	middle	bottles	

Mom cleans and cuts apples. We dip and eat the apples. Yum. We are glad that apples made the trip from farm to table.

56

Is going to the store fun? Supermarkets have rows and rows of jars, bags, and cans. We can get baked rolls, apples, beans, meat, and more at supermarkets.

It takes lots of steps for food to get to our table. These steps start at the farm.

We can get dried apples and apple pies and cakes. We can get apple jellies and apple drinks. We can get just plain apples. We can find them at the store.

Take an apple or two or more. Pay for them. Now we can take apples home.

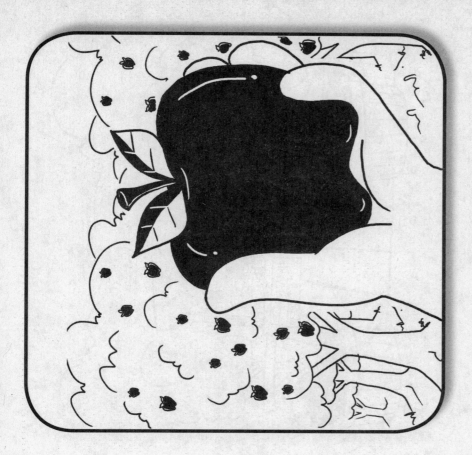

Take an apple. It can be red, yellow, or green. It grows on trees. How did it get from tree to store? The answer is simple.

Start at an apple farm. Apples grow on apple trees. Little apples get bigger and bigger. Big apples get ripe.

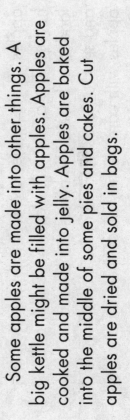

Some apples are made into other things. A big kettle might be filled with apples. Apples are cooked and made into jelly. Apples are baked into the middle of some pies and cakes. Cut apples are dried and sold in bags.

It is time to pick ripe apples. At one farm, we can pick apples right off trees. We can fill a basket and pay for the basket of apples.

At the farm stand while we pay, a big bowl is filled with apple cider. We use the ladle to fill cups. Sip. If we like the sample, we can buy bottles of cider.

52

At most farms, workers are paid to pick apples. These apples are sent to big sorting houses. The apples are cleaned, sorted, and loaded in boxes. The boxes are loaded on trucks and sent to stores. People at the stores handle the apples with care as they place them on a table. Grapes and lemons are on tables as well.

53

The Scarecrow

Written by Sheldon Cline
Illustrated by Anne Rosen

Phonics Skill
Compound Words

scarecrow	roadway	outside	sunshine	rainstorms
peapods	weekend	roadside	anybody	haircut

Dad and Ron drove off. They will be at camp by sunset. Ron smiled at the scarecrow. Ron waved goodbye, and so did the scarecrow!

64

Scarecrow rested on a pole in rows of pea plants near the roadway. He hung outside in sunshine and rainstorms. He waved crows away from the peapods.

Ron and Dad were on their way to Calvin Campgrounds for the weekend. Ron pointed at the scarecrow as Dad drove by. "See it, Dad?" Ron asked. "Can you see it?"

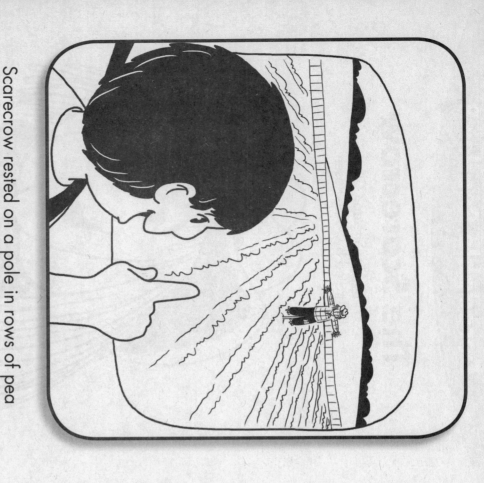

Dad came out of the farmhouse. "We have to wait for help," he told Ron.

"Try it, Dad. I think it will start and run right." Dad started the car and it purred.

"That is funny," Dad noted. "The car is fixed! How did you know, Ron?"

Ron just smiled. It was his secret.

Just as Dad and Ron passed the farm, the car started to tremble and bump down the road. "Oh, no," moaned Dad. "We need to stop. Maybe we can get help at that farmhouse. Stay near the car, Ron."

As Dad made his way to the house, Ron spied wild berries by the roadside. He got out to take some.

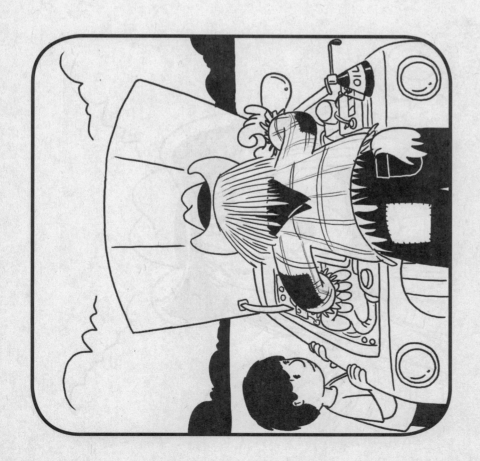

Ron and the scarecrow went to the car. The scarecrow looked at it. He found an oil can. "A little oil here and a little oil there. It is fixed. Now it is time for me to go home." He stumbled to his pole and winked at Ron.

Then Ron heard someone speak, but he did not see anybody. "Who is it? What did you say?" "Do you need help?" the scarecrow asked as he tapped Ron. Ron jumped. "But . . . but," Ron mumbled.

The scarecrow was dressed in rags. He had a pumpkin head, and he had on a cowboy hat. He had long hair made of hay. He needed a haircut! "Let's see if we can fix the car," he said.

His Biggest Fan

Written by Ted Brill
Illustrated by Casey Allen

ANTON

#1

Phonics Skill

Consonant Blends

street	squealed	throw	splendid	spray
thrill	struggle	throat	split	square

Jake smiled at Anton. Anton gave Jake's hand a squeeze.

"It is a thrill to meet you, Anton." Jake grinned from ear to ear.

"No, Jake, the thrill is mine. Meeting my biggest fan makes me happy."

72

"Did you hear?" Kate ran down the street and into the house. "Jake, did you hear? Anton Ford is in town! He is going to sign cards at the sports store on Sunday."

"You must be kidding," Jake squealed. "Anton is the best. He can throw. He hits home runs. I must see him. I am his biggest fan!"

"Jake, this is Anton Ford." Jake could not believe his ears. "I met Kate and found out that you are ill," Anton said.

Jake could just squeak. "Mom, Anton Ford is stopping by to see me. Is that okay?"

"Yes, it is splendid, Jake."

Jake made plans. "I will ask Mom to drive us to the square. There will be a line. I will take my cards. I will take my book about the team as well. I bet Anton will sign it. I will wait and wait. I will wait the whole day. Yes! I would even be willing to wait three days. Seeing Anton is a dream."

"Hello!" Mom answered.
"Hello, is Jake in?"
"Please wait. I will get him," Mom said. "Jake, it is for you."
Jake picked up. "Yes, this is Jake."

Dreaming is just what Jake did. Anton was at bat. He swung. Strike one. Anton tipped the next pitch, but his bat split in two. Strike two. Then Anton hit it hard! Jake squinted to see it fly out of the park. Anton hit a home run. His team greeted him at home plate.

68

Jake woke up. His throat was sore. He had to struggle to get out of bed. Mom said he was hot and sent him back to bed.

"No, Mom, I cannot stay in bed. Anton Ford is here. I need to see him. He can squiggle his name on my cards."

"Kate can go, Jake. You must stay in bed." Jake moaned, "But, Mom, it is Anton. He is the best!"

"No buts. Get in bed now, Jake." Mom said. "Use this spray. It will feel good."

69

Our Running Team

Written by G.B. Kim
Illustrated by Luis Vidal

Phonics Skill

Consonant Digraphs

athlete	champs	pitcher	finish	Michigan
coach	trophy	weather	when	machine

This is the day of our big race! Our team has trained for weeks. Our coach thinks that we will win that trophy if we do our best and help each other. That is our goal. We cannot wait!

80

Shasta, Beth, Cher, and I run each day. We joined the track team together. We train after school. We run even when the weather is wet and cold. We are training for the big race and we hope to be this year's Michigan state champs!

74

I just run because I like it! I think about flying when I am running. It is nice when gentle wind rushes by my ears. Our coach said that helps me run well. When we enjoy our training, we can do our best.

79

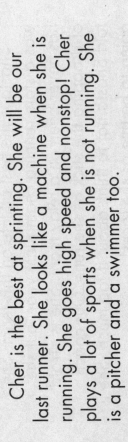

We run on the relay team. In a relay race, runners wait at different places around the track. As one runner races up, she hands a stick to the next runner, who takes off as fast as she can. The last runner sprints for the finish line.

Cher is the best at sprinting. She will be our last runner. She looks like a machine when she is running. She goes high speed and nonstop! Cher plays a lot of sports when she is not running. She is a pitcher and a swimmer too.

Beth is the fastest I have seen. She can take off in a flash—like a rabbit! Beth just came to our class this year, but she fit in well on our team. I am glad she is here. So is the rest of our team! Beth's speed will help our team do well in that race.

Shasta is the best athlete on this team. She was a state running champ last year, but she has never been on a relay team. She is afraid of dropping the stick as she runs. Our coach told Shasta not to think about it too much. She is going to be fine as she races!

The Missing Cap

Written by Leslie Knowles
Illustrated by Brett Andrews

Phonics Skill

Contractions

couldn't	hadn't	let's	we're	I've
wasn't		he'd	you'll	what's	didn't

Phillip just laughed. Now he'd know where to locate missing sunglasses and brushes—under the kitchen sink!

Phillip pulled on his white pants and his red top. He just couldn't wait for today's game. Last night, Phillip hadn't made a single strike. He'd felt pleased when fans in the stands had yelled and clapped. This time Phillip might even hit some home runs!

Phillip's brother came into Phillip's room. "Let's play!" Joe shouted. Joe was just three.

82

Patty pulled out Joe's lunchbox. It had robots on it. "Silly Joe often stores stuff here," Patty said. She opened Joe's lunchbox. There lay Phillip's cap. It looked crushed, but Phillip didn't mind. Hurray! He'd hit those home runs yet!

Just then Joe came in. "It's time to play!" he yelled.

87

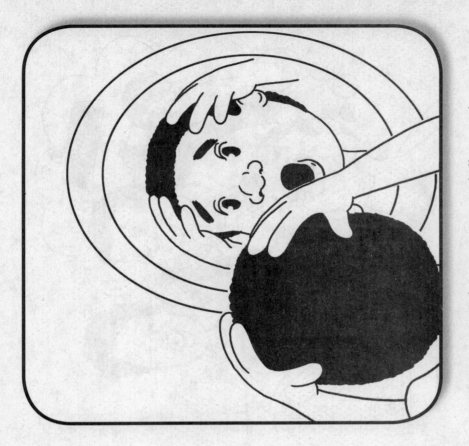

"We're not playing, Joe," Phillip said. "I've got a game in an hour."

Phillip tugged on his long socks. He stopped to look at himself. Wasn't something missing? Phillip scratched his head. His cap! Phillip looked on his bedside stand. His cap wasn't there. He looked on his bed. He looked under it. Where was his cap? Phillip was worried.

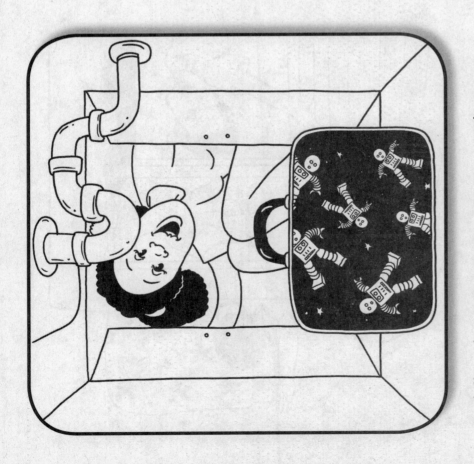

Phillip's big sister Patty came in. "What's everybody looking for?" Patty asked.

"My cap. But I'm sure you can't find it," Phillip said.

"I'll bet I can!" Patty frowned. Then she opened doors under the kitchen sink.

"You're not helping!" Phillip said. "Why would my cap be under the kitchen sink?"

Mom was peeling carrots in the kitchen. She smiled at Phillip. But she hadn't seen his cap.

Mom asked where he'd seen it last.

Phillip pictured his game last night. It was very late. His dad had driven him home. Phillip had gone to bed as soon as he got home. Hadn't he placed his cap on his bedside stand?

"Look in Joe's room," Mom suggested. "I'll look in the car." No cap!

"If you'll look under chairs, I'll look under tables," Mom said. No cap!

"Coach Pepper has a strict rule: team members can't play without caps," Phillip said. "But if I'm late, he'll begin without me." Phillip's day just wasn't going as he'd planned.

Tigers in Trouble

Written by Shane McIntire

Illustrated by Frank Bailey

Phonics Skill

Prefixes un-, re-, mis-, dis-

disappear	unknown	disgrace	recycle	replace
mistreat	unlawfully	reclaim	reuse	unhappy

We can also tell others that we need to save tigers in trouble. We can join a club that fights to save our tigers. If all the tigers die, we can't replace them. Let's try to stop an unhappy ending to this tale.

96

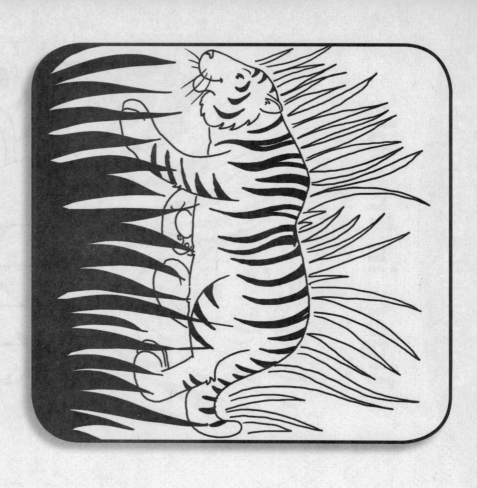

Most of us have not seen tigers in the wild. Tigers pad along in forests. They are white and gold with black stripes. These colors help tigers blend in so they can hide and hunt for food. Such big cats need lots of meat. A tiger can eat 50 pounds of meat in a single meal!

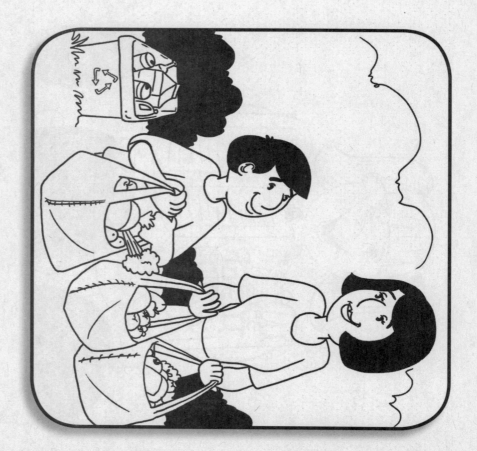

How can we slow cutting of trees? We can save some wild homes for tigers if we cut back on things we buy. We can change our habits.

1. Use less paper.
2. Recycle and reuse.

Tigers are strong and fast. A tiger can leap 30 feet. Look out deer! A tiger roams for miles and miles looking for food.

A tiger makes a den in a cave, a hollow tree, or heavy brush. Most tigers sleep when it's daylight and hunt at night.

We hope the answer is NO! People must not let tigers die out. It would be a mistake and a disgrace. We must try to save our tigers. How?

We can give tigers safe places to live away from people. We can reclaim some land for wild tigers' homes.

94

But now tigers are in trouble. Tigers need land with trees for homes. People cut down trees to build houses and to clear land for growing crops. This means that tiger homes will disappear. Then tigers will not find deer to eat. We may not mean to mistreat tigers, but that is what happens. Tigers can't live with people.

92

Hunters poach, or unlawfully hunt, tigers. There are rules to keep tigers safe. But some people will not follow rules. Each day, tigers die. How many are left is unknown. We think there may be only about 6,000 tigers left in the world. Will tigers die out?

NO HUNTING

93

The Chess Club

Written by Robert Stirim
Illustrated by Beth Fraulini

Phonics Skill

Suffixes -ly, -ful, -ness, -less

illness	careful	cheerful	suddenly	skillful
rapidly	proudly	kindness	beautiful	finally

The day Mike left, his mom went to Travis and gave him her hand.

"Thanks for your kindness to Mike," she said.

"He had a wonderful summer."

Travis was silent. Finally he spoke.

"That's not the way I see it," he said. "It was Mike who showed kindness to me."

104

It had not been the best week for Travis. He had been stuck in bed for six days with a sore throat. Now it was time to try out for the soccer team, but Travis was weak from his illness, and his dad wouldn't let him play.

Travis went outside and kicked and stamped his feet.

Each day that summer, the chess club met in Mike's yard.

Then one day Mike told Travis that he had to move to Boston to be near his new doctor.

"He'll help me get well," Mike said. "Keep on playing chess."

"I will," Travis replied sadly.

"Be careful. You might land on the ground!"

Travis spun around. A boy in a wheelchair was sitting in the next yard. He gave Travis a cheerful smile.

"Why are you so upset?" the boy asked.

Travis was startled. He looked at the boy and scowled. He explained his problem.

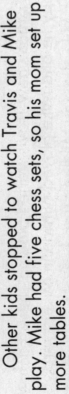

Other kids stopped to watch Travis and Mike play. Mike had five chess sets, so his mom set up more tables.

"Come and play," she told them.

"Now I've got a chess team," Mike boasted proudly.

Travis smiled. "This is not the team I expected to be on," he thought.

Suddenly Travis felt bad. The boy in the chair would never be able to play soccer.

"My name's Travis," he said.

"I'm Mike," the boy replied. "Want to play chess?"

Travis stopped. Chess was for brains.

"Come on, I'll teach you," said Mike.

That's how Travis started playing chess. Each day he and Mike played outside in Mike's yard. Mike was very skillful at chess and beat Travis every time. But Travis rapidly got better and made Mike play hard.

"I must be a brain," Travis admitted one day. "I really like this game."

Stuck in the Mud

Written by Cassie Merin
Illustrated by Nico Sanders

Phonics Skill

g, j, dge /j/; s, c /s/; c, k, ck, ch /k/

| school | ridge | city | cell | track |
| echoed | silly | stuck | voices | large |

When they got there, kids on the bus were not upset. Jake was making silly faces and voices. He was acting out "The Three Little Pigs" by himself. The kids were enjoying his play. Jack and Jake had saved the day.

112

Jack and Jake lived on the ridge far above the city lights. Every morning the twins rode the school bus down the gentle slopes to Oak Trail School on the south edge of town.

After school Jack ran with the track team. Jake went to acting club. He liked being on stage. Then Jack and Jake went home on the bus.

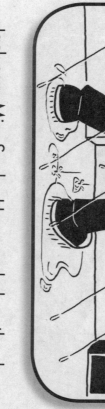

Jack saw Miss Sealy. He pounded on the door. "Jack, you are soaked. Why are you here?" she asked.

Once she heard Jack's story, she phoned for a tow truck. She phoned moms and dads telling them what had happened. She and Jack got in her car. She was sure kids on the bus would be upset.

On this rain-soaked day, Jack and Jake would get a chance to help out by using their track and acting skills. It had rained since morning. Suddenly, hail the size of ice cubes pelted down. Lightning flashed and loud cracks of thunder echoed around the bus.

Jack agreed. "It's not far. I will get help. The school will send a tow truck."

Mr. Ford decided that might be the best plan. He gave Jack a poncho and told him to be careful.

Jack waved and then raced down the hill. He tried to pace himself so that he would not tire out too quickly.

That's when it happened! The bus crossed Old Creek Bridge and then slid. One tire ended up in a large roadside mud puddle. Mr. Ford rocked the bus back and forth, but the tire dug deeper and deeper. It was stuck in mud.

108

Mr. Ford tried his cell phone, but it did not work in storms. He had no way to phone for help. Jake suggested that someone go for help. "Jack is on the track team. He can run back to school."

109

Our Amazing Camp Race

Written by Charis Baronne
Illustrated by Daniel Ibson

Phonics Skill

Silent consonants

| climbing | crumb | designed | gnats | know |
| nestled | rustling | wrist | wrung | knee-deep |

Ben wrestled off his shoes and wrung out his socks. Then he got up and we set off. As we came around a bend, we saw our camp! We ran quickly to reach Stan. He patted us on our backs.

"That is a job well done!" he said proudly. Even Ben with his wet socks grinned at that.

120

Stan whistled so that we would listen. "This path is designed to test your skills," Stan said. Ben, Liz, and Rick were on my team.

"We will use what we know about hiking and camping," Ben said. "We must read signs and check our maps to know where to go."

114

Our next task was to cross the bog on an old rope bridge. But when Ben stepped on that bridge, it broke! Splash! He fell into the muddy bog. When he got up, he was knee-deep in brown muck. He trudged slowly across the bog as Rick, Liz, and I crossed on stepping stones.

119

When Stan whistled again, we were off! We started by climbing up a huge hill. Liz slipped on rocks, but I grabbed her wrist and helped her up. At the top, we found the path. We went into the forest together.

"Listen!" I said quickly. "Can you hear that rustling sound?"

We combed the grass. We found a wren in her nest, with fuzzy chicks nestled under her wings. We went happily back to our trail without bothering those sleepy wrens.

Gnats buzzed around our heads. We waved our hands and brushed them away. Soon, we came to a place where a big tree limb had crashed to the ground.

"That must have happened when the storm came," Rick noted. We wriggled under that limb.

116

Our tired team stopped to eat lunch in silence. When we had finished, not a single crumb was left!

"It is hot and dry," Liz pointed out. "We must drink plenty of liquid."

117

Take-Home

Decodable
Readers
16–30

A Party for the Geese

Written by Kenneth Freid
Illustrated by Joan Autrel

Phonics Skill
Irregular plurals

men	women	children
leaves	geese	wolves
	knives	
	loaves	

After eating, the neighbors watched the geese.
They seemed to enjoy parties too!

8

Each summer the Glendale Street families held a big party. On a bright June day, everybody gladly marched to Blake Pond. Men carried large boxes filled with cold drinks. Women carried big baskets and bags filled with lunch, plates, cups, forks, and knives. Children carried gear for playing games.

The pond looked peaceful. Soft breezes ruffled leaves. Ducks floated on the pond. Big, loud geese waded by the water.

2

"I think Mrs. Wong has been really helpful," Mr. Perez said. "Now those geese can have their own meal. They will let us enjoy our party!"

The families ate salads, chicken, potatoes, pickles, peaches, and apples. Everybody enjoyed lunch.

7

"Let's play a game," Jeff Sanders suggested. "We've got plenty of people for two teams."

"We can leave lunch on the tables," Mrs. Perez said.

"I'm not playing," Mrs. Wong said, "so I will set up the tables."

"But let me tell you what happened. I was just taking bags of crackers and loaves of bread to the tables. Seven geese came running, honking loudly. More followed them. I tripped over geese. I waved bags to make them leave, but then a bag broke. Crackers and bread tumbled out. I got upset, but those silly geese seemed really happy!" Everybody laughed. Mrs. Wong felt fine. They still had plenty of lunch for everybody.

The neighbors played a lively game. One team scored six runs. The other team scored seven runs.

"I'm starved!" Kelly Wong finally yelled. "It's lunchtime!"

Men, women, and children quickly went back to the tables. Then everybody saw a strange sight.

Mrs. Wong stood near the tables looking unhappy. Crackers and loaves of bread lay nearby. Seven geese honked loudly.

Everybody spoke at the same time. "What happened? What's going on? Where's lunch?"

Mrs. Wong laughed. "It looks as if wild wolves chased me. But it was really just these geese," she said.

Whirling Girl

Written by Jennifer Hills
Illustrated by Anita Morelli

© Pearson Education 3

Phonics Skill

R-controlled /ėr/: ir, er, ur, ear, or

whirling	early	word	hurled	certain
world	Turkey	dirt	earth	pearls

© Pearson Education 3

Shirley learned to skate so well, she became a star. She liked her skating dress with pearls and sequins. She sparkled as she leaped and danced over the ice. But the crowd enjoyed it most when Shirley, the Whirling Girl, twirled like a top.

Shirley had talent. From the beginning her parents saw that she was going places. Early in the morning on the day after her birth, Shirley began to whirl. Mom and Dad found her spinning like a top in her crib.

"What on Earth!" exclaimed Dad.

"My word!" cried Mom.

At last they had it! "Come with us, Shirley," said Mom and Dad. They drove to an ice rink. Shirley tied on ice skates.

"Meet Coach Durning," said Mom. "She will teach you to skate."

Shirley learned to soar like a bird over the ice.

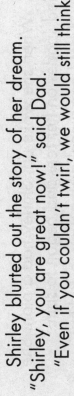

Shirley was a happy baby. She became a sweet girl who liked helping out. She was happiest when spinning. She learned to use her spinning in lots of ways. She gave kids airplane rides. She hurled the shot put about a mile. Shirley could hang paintings quicker than a blink.

Shirley blurted out the story of her dream.

"Shirley, you are great now!" said Dad.

"Even if you couldn't twirl, we would still think you are great," added Mom.

But Shirley felt so sad that Mom and Dad began thinking. Their thinking went round and round.

But Shirley was certain she could do more. How could a talent for spinning help the world? Shirley dreamed a dream. In her dream, she became Whirling Girl! She bored a hole into the earth and saved a lost boy. She whirled rope around men who were robbing First Bank and left them in a neat bundle.

When she woke up, Shirley had a plan. She tied spades on her feet and began to spin.
"I bet I can tunnel all the way to Turkey!"
Her tunnels were huge wormholes.
"There is a lot of dirt in this yard," yelled Dad.
"What were you thinking?" asked Mom.

A Pole Bean Tent

Written by Neil Fairbairn
Illustrated by Lena Bartolai

Phonics Skill

Prefixes pre-, mid-, over-, out-

outdoors	outline	outside	midpoint	presoak
overcrowded	midsummer	overgrown	overhead

Your bean tent is like a house with leaves and flowers growing overhead. It is a place for shade on a hot day. It is a place to play hide-and-seek or just sit inside and read.

And it has plenty of green beans to pick and eat!

24

Do you have a green thumb? Then try gardening for a fun way to spend time outdoors. You can get lots of fresh air—and things to eat. Think about what you can grow: peas, peppers, carrots, berries, and more.

I think beans are best. You can eat them and play with them as well. That's right, play with them. Here's how.

By midsummer your bean plants will reach pole tops. The frame will be overgrown with big leaves and bright flowers. These flowers will turn into beans you can eat.

Now can you see why you left space between two poles? It's an opening for your pole bean tent!

First, go to a garden shop and pick up a packet of pole bean seeds. Also get six thin poles, each at least six feet long.

Next, set up the planting space in the garden. On the ground, outline a circle three feet wide. Then pull weeds and turn over the dirt inside the circle with a garden fork.

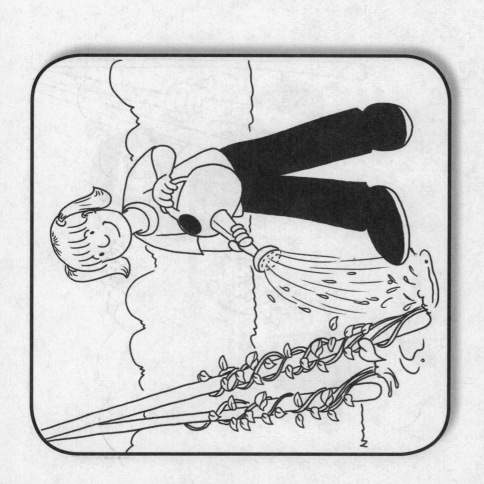

When the bean plants are three inches high, thin them out. Take out the little ones, and leave three strong plants at each pole. The plants must not be overcrowded.

Keep sprinkling them with water, and see how fast they grow. Your plants will race up the poles.

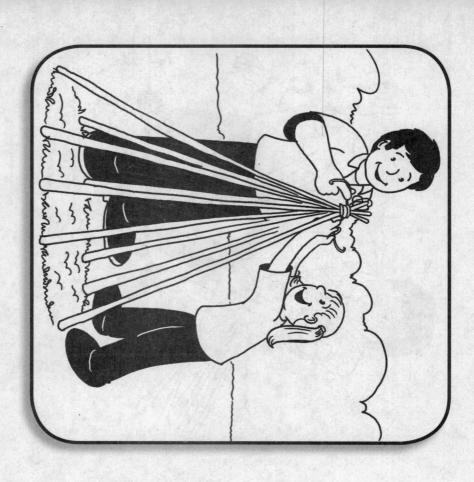

Rake the ground flat. Then place six poles around the outside of the circle with their tops leaning into the midpoint. Leave a bigger space between two poles. Why? Wait and see!

Tie the pole tops with string. Now you've got a pole frame.

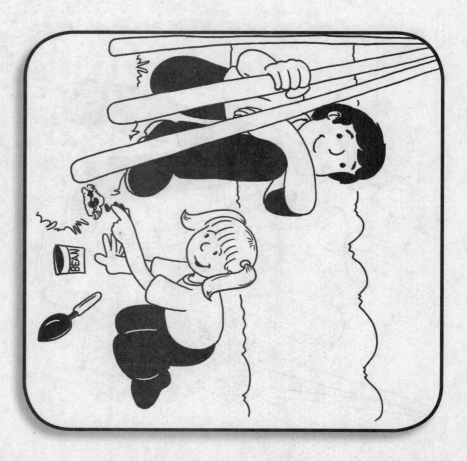

When days start getting hot in late spring, presoak your bean seeds. Plant them by placing six beans at the base of each pole and poking them an inch into the ground. Place dirt over them and water them daily.

In less than ten days, your bean plants will sprout.

Teller, Tailor, Seller, Sailor

Written by K. E. Theroux
Illustrated by James Connor

NURSE? ACTOR?

DENTIST?

TEACHER?

ARTIST?

Phonics Skill

Suffixes -er, -or, -ess, -ist

actress	artist	chemist	conductor	inventor
firefighter	editor	seller	driver	sailor

FIREFIGHTER!
NURSE!
WRITER!
ACTRESS!
CONDUCTOR!
DENTIST!
TEACHER!
PILOT!
INVENTOR!
CHEMIST!

"Now, class," said Miss Lim. "Let's start writing. Has everybody picked a job?"

"Actress! Writer! Dentist! Inventor! Firefighter! Nurse! Conductor! Pilot! Chemist! TEACHER!"

Miss Lim smiled and held up her hands. "My, you're eager to write about your jobs! Now let's see that in your writing."

32

"Now we'll discuss jobs," Miss Lim told her class on Friday morning after math. "We know that jobs are things that people do for a living, so first tell me what my job is."

Lola spoke quickly, "You're a teacher, Miss Lim."

"And what do teachers do?" asked Miss Lim.

"Teachers help us learn things," Jeb finally blurted out.

First, Jeb sees himself as a racecar driver. He sees a sleek car speeding on a racetrack, and he holds the wheel tightly as he wins the race!

Then Jeb sees himself as a teacher. He sees happy kids sitting in a classroom, and he helps them learn things—just like Miss Lim!

"Now think about more jobs that people do when they grow up," Miss Lim said, handing out paper.

"After picking one job, you'll write about that job and tell why you picked it." Little by little the room grew silent as the class started making lists of jobs.

Zan likes reading stories. Editors fix mistakes in stories before they get printed, so an editor will read lots of stories.

Zan likes listening to music. Conductors lead bands when they play, so a conductor will listen to lots of music. Which job would be better for him?

30

Rose can see herself in two jobs. First, she is an artist, and she paints big red flowers and yellow suns on large white canvases. People admire her bright paintings.

Then she is an actress, and she speaks her lines in plays on stage without making a single mistake! People clap and whistle loudly for her.

Lola knows she wants a job in which she helps people.

Her uncle is a doctor, and her mom is a dentist. Lola has watched them both at work. Doctors help sick or hurt people, while dentists help people care for their teeth. Both are fine jobs, and both jobs help people. Which job should she pick?

A Plan Is Hatched

Written by Julie Renault
Illustrated by Leslie Sidon

Phonics Skill

Syllable pattern VCCCV

complain	constant	exclaimed	hungry	inspect
impressed	instant	Mildred	monster	surprise

"It was such fun to help with that big bird," Constance said. "So now I am planning a huge ranch myself, with at least a hundred ostriches!"

Sandra was impressed by Constance's grand plan. "That's exciting!" Sandra exclaimed. "It sounds like fun."

"So, Sandra," Constance added with a wink, "do you want to help me work with the ostriches?"

40

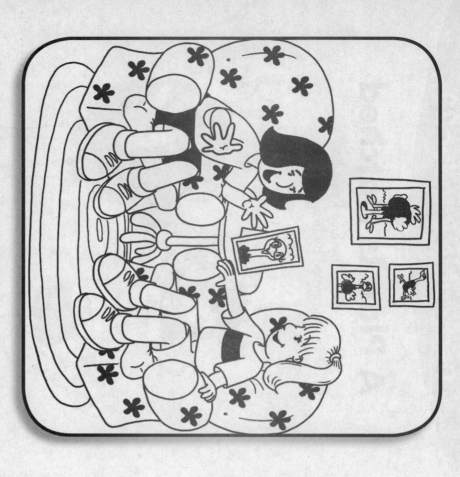

Constance has a big dream. Her friends think it is a very strange dream. In fact, they think her plan is a little bird-brained. That's because Constance plans to own an ostrich farm!

"An ostrich farm?" Sandra asked. "Last time we talked you were going to be an actress!"

"That's a long story," Constance replied. She then told Sandra her long ostrich tale.

"Maybe it's hungry. When did it last eat?" I asked Miss Mildred, edging slowly closer.

Uncle Clem had sent big food bags with this crate. We gave that ostrich a nice snack. In an instant he was quiet. He made happy little sounds as he gobbled his food.

One day I heard an odd noise outside. That constant, loud noise went on and on, and soon I couldn't stand it a moment longer. I went to my window to complain. Little did I know as I opened the window that my goal in life would change.

I went out to inspect Miss Mildred's "monster." When I peeked in the noisy crate, I got a complete surprise.

"It's an ostrich!" I shouted, jumping back in shock.

"Yes," Miss Mildred moaned, shaking her head. "Please, can you help me with it?"

Miss Mildred, the lady next door, had a huge crate in her yard. That knocking, banging noise came from inside her crate!

"Miss Mildred," I yelled over the racket. "Why is so much noise coming from that crate?"

The banging inside Miss Mildred's crate got louder.

Miss Mildred was in a state of distress! She was so frustrated that she burst into tears.

"Constance, my dear," she replied. "I don't know how to handle this mess! This monster is a birthday gift sent by my crazy Uncle Clem, but I cannot do a single thing to control it!"

Miss Mildred slumped down sadly on her knees.

Radio Days

Written by Corey Tenon
Illustrated by Clarisse Fontana

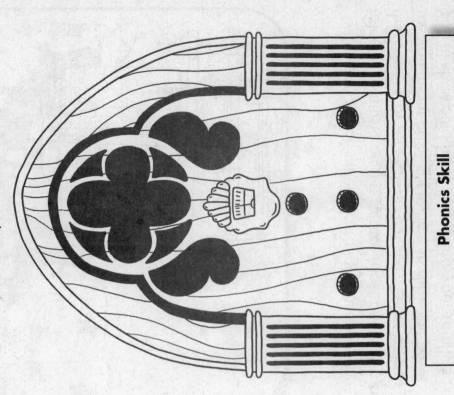

Phonics Skill
Syllable pattern CVVC

audio	created	ideas	pianos	radio
stereo	video	violins	pioneers	scientists

During the Second World War, radio gave audiences daily war news. Then big changes took place in the 1950s. Audiences began turning to TV. Music, news, and sports still aired on radio. But radio's golden age had ended.

48

Did you watch videos last night? Maybe you listened to music on the stereo. Most people enjoy these forms of recreation. But sixty years ago or so, you might have spent time in different ways. You likely would have listened to your family's radio.

Radio shows delighted audiences. In the daytime, children listened to shows made for kids. At night, families laughed at comic shows. Jack Benny and Bob Hope were well-known radio comics. Later, these comics became TV stars.

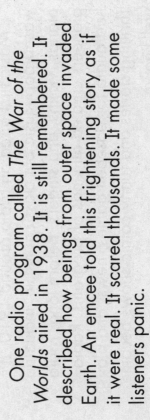

Back in those days, radio didn't just air music or news. Families gathered around big radios in their living rooms each night. They listened happily as actors and actresses performed plays, acted out stories, and cracked jokes. Sound effects made radio plays seem real.

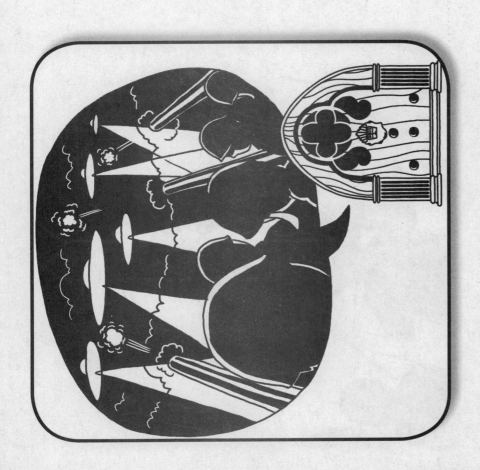

One radio program called *The War of the Worlds* aired in 1938. It is still remembered. It described how beings from outer space invaded Earth. An emcee told this frightening story as if it were real. It scared thousands. It made some listeners panic.

How did radio start? Phones were invented in 1876. Phone signals went through wires. Scientists thought air, not wires, could carry radio signals. An inventor sent radio signals through air in 1895. Soon ships at sea could make calls with radios. Radio helped save shipwreck victims.

Before long, airplane pilots and armies used radios. Everybody called radio the wireless since radio waves moved through air without wires.

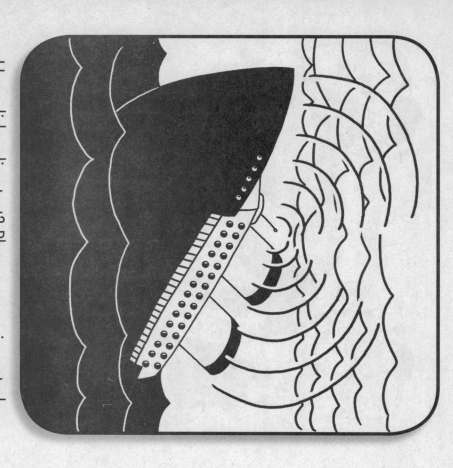

Music first aired on radio around 1910. It wasn't pop music but classical music, including pianos, violins, and singers. Before long, radio pioneers created all kinds of programs. Radio had audio for baseball games, news, and plays. Thrilling stories and funny comic shows became well-known.

All Week Long

Written by Hilda Zadylak
Illustrated by Lily Goucher

Phonics Skill

Homophones

| board/bored | flour/flower | here/hear | road/rode |
| role/roll | stair/stare | week/weak | write/right |

It had been a fun-filled week without even an echo of "I'm bored."

In her diary, Val would write, "The world is full of sounds, smells, tastes, feelings, and sights."

On Saturday, Val went outside first thing. She was sure the world had many more things to teach her, and she was right!

56

"I'm bored," Val said to Mom. "What can I do?"

It was the middle of summer. Val tapped her fingers on the board her mom was painting.

"Look at the world around you," said Mom.

"Stop and take time to observe, and you will not be bored."

"How can I begin?" asked Val.

50

Friday was a day for seeing. Val and Aunt Lin strolled to the park. There were many things to stare at. Standing on a stair, Val watched a line of ants. Each ant held bits of leaves. Next Val and Aunt Lin sat down and watched a ballgame for an hour. It ended when a player struck out.

"Our day was fun!" Val told Mom when she returned home.

55

"What do you hear?" asked Mom. "Listen hard!"

Val did not hear too much at first. At last noises came to her ears. Far away, cars whizzed along. Their motors hummed. Close by, birds sang songs and two bees buzzed. Mom's paintbrush made a whishing noise. Now here came a purring kitten. There were so many sounds to hear.

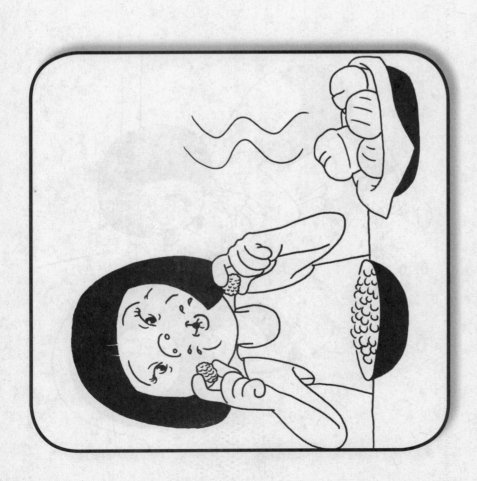

Next Val tried out her taste buds. She played the role of a chef taste-testing foods. She crunched peanuts and chips. She tried pickles.

The banana she ate was sweet like cream, but a tart berry exploded in her mouth. She put jam on a hot fresh roll. That tasted best of all.

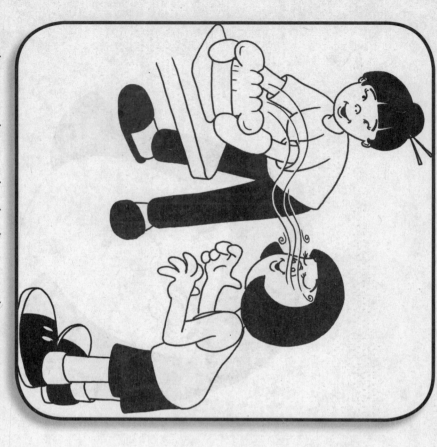

The next day, Val asked, "Now how can I observe?"

Mom knew what to ask. "What can you smell?"

Val sniffed the air. "Nothing," she said. But she found many new things to smell. One flower smelled like spice. Later Mom and Val mixed flour into cake batter. The freshly baked cake would smell sweet.

The next day as they rode in the car, Val grinned and asked, "What now?"

"What can you feel?" asked Mom.

The car seat felt hot. The glass window felt slick. Stones in the road felt sharp. Her puppy's nose was wet and cold. His fur felt soft and warm. Val liked how he felt.

All That Moms Do

Written by Elena Placido
Illustrated by Janice Fairbanks

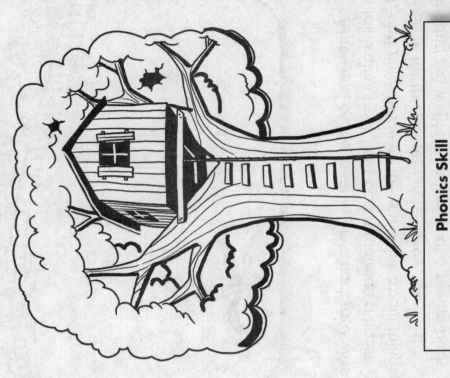

Phonics Skill

Vowel sound in ball: a, au, aw, al

| all | awful | because | lawn | squawk |
| tall | walnut | saw | small | always |

"What's your room like?" asked his mom.

"Go see it," said Jim.

Jim's mom came back a moment later.

"Wow, Jim! What made you clean it?" she asked.

"A little bird told me to," Jim exclaimed.

64

At the end of the lawn in Jim's backyard was a tall walnut tree. Jim's dad had made a house in it, and Jim often went there to think about things. High in his treehouse, Jim felt okay. He liked hearing the wind in the leaves and seeing birds flutter from branch to branch.

Jim got down from the tree and returned to his house. Without a sound he went up to his room and picked up his toys. Then he cleaned up the mess on his bed and desk.

When he had finished, Jim went to find his mom. She was making lunch.

"I'm starving," Jim told her.

One day Jim went to his treehouse because he did not want to clean his room.

"Your room is an awful mess," Mom had said.

"I want you to clean it by lunchtime!"

"No! No! No!" Jim had said to himself. "It's my room, and I like it this way!"

He ran to his treehouse.

"I'll stay here for ten years," Jim said.

The big bird came and went and came and went. Jim counted thirteen trips in all. Each time she came, she gave her baby another meal.

"That mom works hard," Jim said to himself. And suddenly he began thinking about his own mom.

"My mom works hard also. She feeds me just like that mother bird feeds her small baby."

Jim sat in the tree and gazed at his house.

"Mom is always asking me to clean my room or make my bed," he grumbled to himself.

Just then, Jim heard a sound.

"Chirp, chirp, chirp."

Jim saw a baby bird in a nest, calling for food.

A moment later a big bird landed beside the baby.

"This must be its mom," Jim decided.

The mother bird filled her baby's mouth with food.

The little bird gobbled up its dinner. Then it started squawking again.

Mother bird went off to find more food.

Daughters and Moms

Written by Matt Kooper
Illustrated by Bill Franklin

Phonics Skill

Vowel sound in ball: augh, ough

bought	caught	daughter	fought	ought
sought	taught	thought	brought	

They even talked about clothes and meals and bedtimes and baby-sitters. By the time Mom was well, Paula and Mom were getting along fine. And they never disagreed again. Well, maybe they still disagreed, but only now and then. Overall, they began to see eye to eye.

72

Paula and her mom did not always see eye to eye. They had different ideas about clothes and meals. They fought over bedtimes and baby-sitters. They did not like listening to the same CDs. They seemed to disagree about many things.

Mom couldn't make lunches, so Paula bought her lunch in the lunchroom every day. She walked Dawg twice a day and fed him. She taught her mom some awful jokes. Mom told her some almost funny stories. They spent a lot of time together. Paula talked and Mom listened. Mom talked and Paula listened.

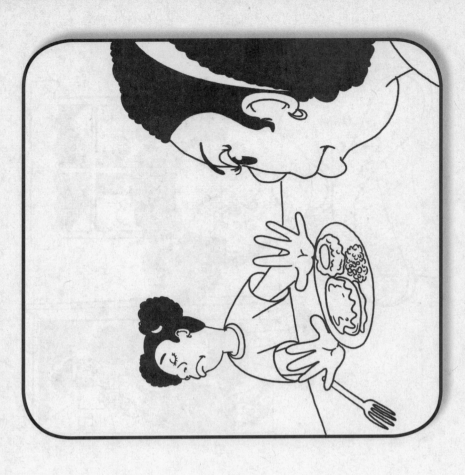

Paula bought a yellow and purple shawl. Her mom said Paula did not need it and had to take it back to the mall. Paula thought that wasn't fair at all.

Mom made meat loaf with brown sauce for dinner. Her daughter ate one bite and balked. She thought it was awful and did not want to eat it. Mom told Paula to eat her dinner.

Mom told her daughter that she was sick and needed Paula's help. Now Paula had many jobs. First she brought her mom hot tea and oatmeal in the morning. Then she greeted Miss Fraught, the home helper, and let her into the house. Paula made her bed and washed the dishes before she walked to the bus stop.

Mom said that Paula's bedtime on weekends was nine. She caught Paula watching TV at ten.

Paula thought she ought to be able to stay at home on her own when Mom went out. But Mom always brought in a baby-sitter. And that's how things went day after day. Paula and Mom almost never talked because they always seemed to disagree.

One day Mom had a cough. It didn't seem like a big deal, but the cough got worse and worse. Finally, Mom sought help from a doctor. He told her that she needed rest and ought to stay in bed resting for two weeks.

Later that day, Mom called to Paula. "We need to talk."

Selfish Shelly

Written by Stephen Grantland
Illustrated by Deborah Cahill

Phonics Skill

Suffixes -y, -ish, -hood, -ment

sunny	childish	childhood	enjoyment	icy
selfish	refreshment	salty	stylish	treatment

Matt saw that she looked sad. He came to her side. "I have been selfish," Shelly told him. "I will try to think of others from now on."

Matt stuck out his hand and helped her up. "You're still our friend," he said. "We can make room at the table for you."

There was room, and Shelly did have fun. After that, she tried hard not to be so selfish.

80

Shelly was a good girl, but she was a little spoiled. She almost always got what she wanted. When she asked for shiny new toys, she got them. When she asked for a frisky little puppy, she got it. When she asked for stylish dresses, she got them. She thought she had a very happy childhood.

74

Shelly sat down on the rocky ground. First she felt grumpy, but then she began to think. "I acted childish and rude," Shelly admitted to herself. "My friends did not like the bad treatment I gave them. I wish I had been kinder. If I had, right now I'd be having fun with them!"

79

On a sunny day in June, Matt had a party for the enjoyment of all the kids in his neighborhood. When the big day came, Shelly wore her sundress made of wispy, yellowish fabric. She came late, so everyone had to wait for her before they could start playing games.

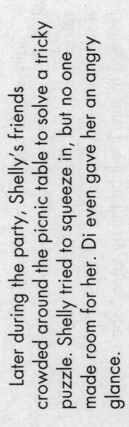

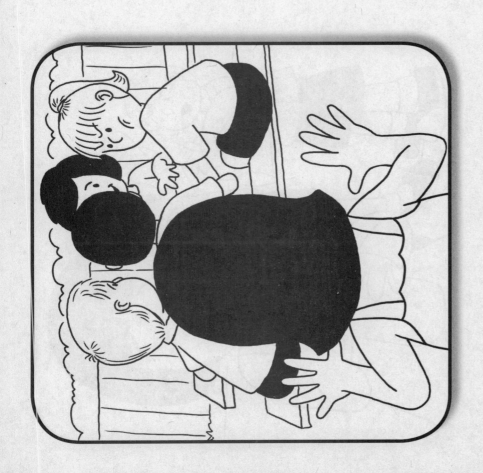

Later during the party, Shelly's friends crowded around the picnic table to solve a tricky puzzle. Shelly tried to squeeze in, but no one made room for her. Di even gave her an angry glance.

Matt had a big tray of snacks. He had crunchy nuts, buttery popcorn, chips and cheesy dip, and sticky apple treats.

"I don't like any of that stuff," Shelly said with a sniff. "I'd rather eat something more healthful."

Matt was sad that he had not made Shelly happy.

Salty snacks and warm sun made the kids thirsty. They went looking for icy cold refreshment. But Shelly had taken all the water, down to the very last drop. "Well, I filled my bottle. I'm sure I will be thirsty later," she said.

Black and White and Big All Over

Written by Callie Terote
Illustrated by Lee Braden

© Pearson Education 3

© Pearson Education 3

"That's true," Sue nodded. "Lots of bamboo trees grow in China where pandas live. Pandas chew bamboo shoots, or tiny branches. They chew bamboo leaves as well. Aren't pandas picky? Bamboo's the only food they'll put in their mouths."

Soon everybody got back on the bus. "Now we all know which animal you like best, Josh," said Brooke. She gave Josh a high five. "Cool!"

88

Josh dressed quickly. His long wait was almost over! Today was his class trip to City Zoo.

At nine sharp, a big school bus parked at Cook School. Josh and Brooke got on first. Soon everybody else joined them. Some children began playing wildly. Cooper jumped up on his seat. Ashley shouted loudly. Josh wasn't unruly. He just wanted to focus on zoo sights he'd see.

"It's not a raccoon or a bear, but it has traits of both. It's a giant panda! Which food do you think Pete Panda likes most?" Sue asked.

"Fruit?" Kevin asked. Sue shook her head.

"Meat? Noodles?" Jane asked. Sue shook her head twice.

"Leaves from a lilac bush?" Kate asked.

Josh just had to speak up. "Bamboo," he said.

"Quiet, please!" Miss Rooney called.

At last Josh and Brooke could hear themselves think.

"I'm excited about seeing tigers," Brooke said happily. "They're the animals I like best. Which do you like best, Josh?"

At long last Sue led everybody to the animal Josh liked best. Just as Josh had hoped, it sat outdoors. It was black and white and quite big. A big black mark circled each eye.

"It looks like a large raccoon!" Martin shouted.

"It looks like a gentle grizzly bear!" Ginny yelled.

"You will find out soon," Josh replied. He smiled shyly at Brooke. Josh didn't really like keeping secrets. But talking too much about the animal might bring bad luck. He hoped he'd find it playing outside. Last time, the animal had hidden in its cool, dark cave. Josh could hardly see his furry friend.

At City Zoo, a helpful zookeeper named Sue greeted Miss Rooney's class. She began showing the excited children zoo animals. They saw lions, tigers, camels, and monkeys. Josh liked them all. At each stop, Brooke asked, "Isn't that the animal you like best, Josh?" Each time, Josh replied, "No."

A Circus Life for Ben

Written by Jenna Borman

Illustrated by Stefan Korzak

Phonics Skill

Unaccented syllables/Word parts

around	circus	family	item	seven
tickets	breakfast	afraid	juggled	moment

Mama and Papa were happy to see Ben. While they fixed breakfast, he told them all about life in the circus. Mama and Papa smiled happily and didn't seem surprised at all.

"Now will you stay home with us, Ben?" they asked.

"Yes," said Ben. "Home is the place for me!"

96

Long ago a family of bears lived in Berry Woods. There was Mama Bear, Papa Bear, and little Harry Benjamin Bear. It was a big name for a tiny bear. But Ben, as everybody called him, had big dreams.

Life was quiet in Berry Woods. It was way too quiet, if you asked Ben!

Ben traveled everywhere with the circus. Its train chugged over mountains and into valleys. The circus went around the world. Ben was a hot item! Tickets sold out in Paris and Rome and Calcutta.

But Ben missed Mama and Papa Bear. He felt sad. "I must go home," he cried. And that is what he did.

Ben wanted to travel around the world. He dreamed about sailing the seven seas. He would zip over bright blue water and see huge whales spout. He dreamed of climbing Earth's tallest mountain. He would plant his family's flag on it. He dreamed of exploring the darkest jungle. All wild animals would be afraid of him.

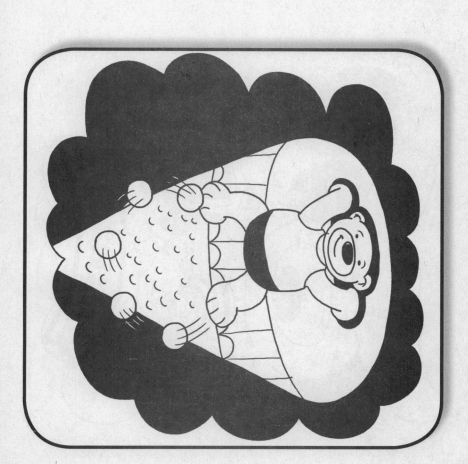

Ben was a hit at the circus. He balanced on his head and juggled balls with his feet.

He swung gracefully on a trapeze. He let go, and the crowd gasped. At just the right moment, he grabbed his swing. Ben was safe!

He climbed into a tiny truck with a clown, and they drove around, honking the horn. Everybody cheered wildly. "Hurray for Ben!"

Then one day, Ben saw a poster. "A circus!" cried Ben. The Flying Bear Circus was coming to Berry Woods!

Ben liked everything about circuses. Now he dreamed about being a high-wire performer or a trapeze artist. He also dreamed about being a famous clown. A circus life was the life for Ben.

92

Ben thought, "I must join the circus!"

Ben packed his lucky marble and some honey. He tiptoed out of his house so Mama and Papa Bear would not wake up. He walked until he was tired. After a little rest, he reached the circus.

"We have been waiting for you," said the Circus Master.

93

Uncle Mycroft

Written by Andy Basset
Illustrated by Sarah Shwall

Phonics Skill

Common syllables -tion, -sion, -ture

adventure	direction	furniture	mansion
potion	questions	station	vacation

At the end of the week, Brad and Ella told Uncle Mycroft that they'd visit him again whenever he needed them.

Mom and Dad met the kids at the bus station.

"Tell us all about your adventure," Dad said.

"What's Uncle Mycroft like now?"

"Well, right now he's kind of like you," Ella said, "but a little shorter."

104

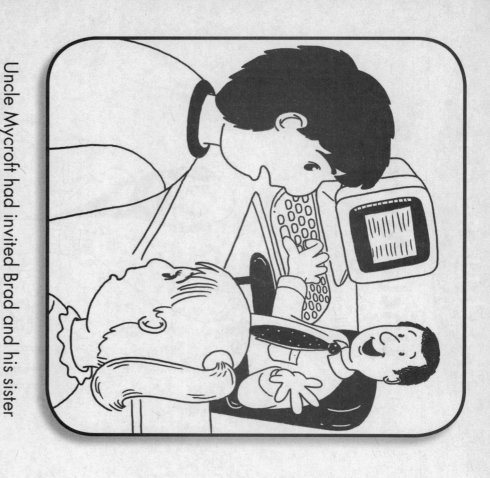

Uncle Mycroft had invited Brad and his sister Ella to spend a week with him. Brad and Ella had never met Uncle Mycroft, and they had lots of questions. Why did he ask to see them now? What was he like? How did he earn his living?

"My brother Mycroft is an inventor," Dad explained. "I speak to him by phone all the time, but I haven't seen him for twenty years."

98

Brad and Ella gasped. Where was Uncle Mycroft this time?

"Look down, kids," called a cheerful voice. They looked down and there was Uncle Mycroft. Yes, they could see him now. But he was just six inches tall.

"Not perfect, but a good start," said the tiny uncle.

103

This would be their first trip without Mom and Dad. They could not get away from work so Ella and Brad traveled alone by bus.

They got a big surprise when they saw Uncle Mycroft's house. His house was an old mansion surrounded by huge trees.

Brad sighed, and Ella took a deep breath and rang the bell.

All that week Brad and Ella went shopping for Uncle Mycroft. And all that week he tested his new potion.

At last it was ready. Uncle Mycroft took a large spoonful. Nothing happened.

Suddenly Brad and Ella heard a small voice. "It worked—well, sort of."

The door creaked open, but no one was in sight. All Brad and Ella saw was a room full of dusty furniture.

"I'm over here, children," said a deep voice. Brad and Ella looked in the direction of the voice. They saw an empty armchair.

"Don't be alarmed," said the voice. "You can't see me because I'm invisible!"

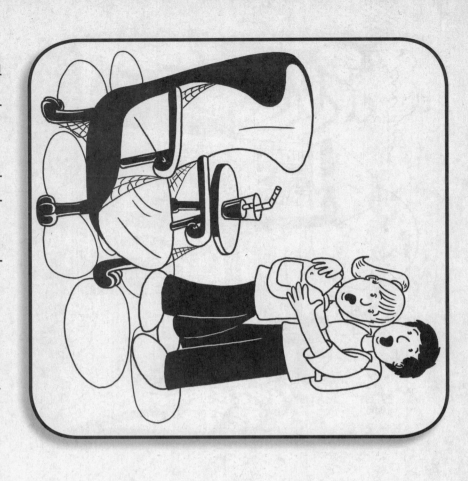

So that was why no one had seen Uncle Mycroft for twenty years!

A long time ago he had invented a potion that made a person invisible. The potion worked perfectly. But Uncle Mycroft had not found a way to reverse it. He wanted Brad and Ella to buy the things he needed for more tests.

The Disappearing Cat

Written by J. A. Vezzetti

Illustrated by Sean Baskin

© Pearson Education 3

Word Structure

Multisyllabic words using word parts

carefully	disliked	hopelessness	reappeared
replacement	unbearably	unhappiest	unprepared

© Pearson Education 3

Suddenly Chase reappeared in the yard.
Unprepared for this sight, Henry didn't move.
Then he grabbed and hugged the cat tightly.
Chase squirmed free and licked his ruffled fur.
He looked at Henry as if to say, "How about refreshments?"

Henry smiled and refilled the food and water dishes. Chase was home.

112

Henry Tucker was the unhappiest boy in Port Town. His cat Chase had disappeared six weeks ago. At first Henry wasn't worried. Chase often got the urge to wander, but he always reappeared in a few days. Henry thought that Chase would have lots of good stories to tell about his trips—if only Chase could talk!

Cat ownership was often hard and messy, but all that Henry recalled now was Chase purring and rubbing on his legs. Henry had disliked it when Chase misbehaved. Now Henry wished that Chase would come back and misbehave as much as he wanted. Henry slumped lower on the steps. He was filled with fear and hopelessness.

After Chase had been gone for three days, Henry started searching for him. First he looked carefully in all the places that Chase might hide. Chase wasn't in the shed in the garden or in the maple tree by the fence. He wasn't under the porch of the red house on Vine Street.

Henry thought about Chase all the time. He recalled that Chase often sat on Henry's desk while he worked. Chase gracefully tucked his paws and watched Henry with big green eyes. Now the desk looked impossibly empty. At night in bed Chase would curl up right next to Henry. It was a bit uncomfortable at first, but Henry got used to it. Now his bed felt unbearably lonely.

Chase wasn't in the boxes behind the bookstore or by the food market. He wasn't in the tall grass or under the hedges around the pond.

Next Henry posted signs all over town. The signs had the word *Missing*, a picture of Chase, and a phone number. Henry waited by the phone, but no one called.

As the days went by, Henry grew discouraged. His dad took him to the animal pound. There were lots of cats there, but no Chase. Dad said, not unkindly, "Maybe you want to get another cat."

A replacement for Chase? That idea was unacceptable to Henry. Chase was much too remarkable a cat.

Mike the Medic

Written by Renee McLean

Illustrated by Kourtney Garret

Phonics Skill		
Related words		
act/action	breath/breathe	cloth/clothes	sign/signal
hand/handle	medic/medical	safe/safety	finally/finished

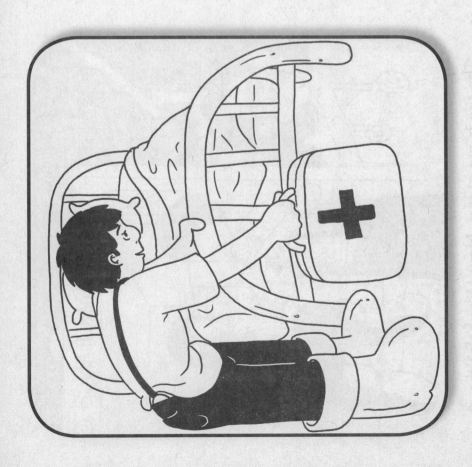

When they are finished, Mike and the other firefighters return to the station. Mike can finally get back to sleep. He is really tired now, but he is also happy that he is able to do such good work. His ability to help people every day makes Mike very proud.

120

This is Mike. He is a medic. A medic helps people who have medical problems before they can get to a doctor. Mike gives first aid when people are hurt or sick. Medics help take injured or sick people to the hospital so that they can get medicine and other help needed.

The fire is out at last. Now Mike helps the firefighters. Tim feels sick from heat and smoke. He cannot catch his breath. Mike puts a mask on his face to help him breathe clean air while he rests. Tim will see a doctor to make sure he is healthy and safe. Marla needs Mike's help too. She fell inside the house and cut her arm. Mike works hard looking after these brave safety workers.

Mike works for the fire department. Like many medics, he is a firefighter too. Mike sleeps at the firehouse. But Mike won't stay asleep for long. The alarm tells Mike that it is time to wake up and get to work. He gets dressed quickly and rushes to his truck. It's time for action!

Mike sees a family standing on the sidewalk. They look cold and frightened. Their clothes smell smoky and their faces are sooty. But everybody is safe. They had put cloth over their noses and mouths, which protected them from smoke. Mike checks them out and wraps blankets around them to keep them warm.

The truck has lights and sirens that signal drivers to pull over to the side of the road. Bright, flashing lights and loud, wailing sirens are signs that this truck needs to get someplace fast. Cars pull over and stop to make way for this fire truck.

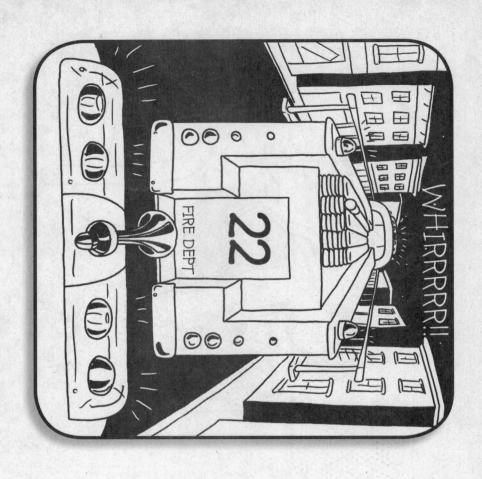

WHIRRRR!!

116

When the truck gets to the place where help is needed, the firefighters see smoke. A house is on fire! Mike and the other firefighters act quickly. Mike grabs the handle of his first-aid kit with one hand and blankets with his other hand. While other firefighters put the fire out, Mike checks to see if anyone is hurt.

117